Simple Watercol
Backgrounds for Scrapbooks

Polly Pinder

Oscar's first *sandy bottom* experience

Dominic bowling for England

Beside the Seaside

Poppa with the little Pinders by the chilly North Sea

SEARCH PRESS

First published in Great Britain 2005

Search Press Limited
Wellwood, North Farm Road,
Tunbridge Wells, Kent TN2 3DR

Text copyright © Polly Pinder 2005

Photographs by Roddy Paine Photographic Studios
Photographs and design copyright © Search Press Ltd 2005

ISBN 1 84448 074 7

The Publishers and author can accept no responsibility for any
consequences arising from the information, advice or instructions
given in this publication.

Readers are permitted to reproduce any of the items/patterns in
this book for their personal use, or for the purposes of selling for
charity, free of charge and without the prior permission of the
Publishers. Any use of the items/patterns for commercial
purposes is not permitted without the prior permission of
the Publishers.

Suppliers
If you have difficulty in obtaining any of the materials and
equipment mentioned in this book, then please write to the
Publishers, at the address above, for a current list of stockists,
including firms who operate a mail-order service.

Publisher's note
All the step-by-step photographs in this book feature the
author, Polly Pinder, demonstrating watercolour painting for
scrapbooks. No models have been used.
   There are references to animal hair brushes in this book. It
is the publishers' custom to recommend synthetic materials
as substitutes for animal products wherever possible. There
is now a large range of brushes available made from artificial
fibres, and they are satisfactory substitutes for those made
from natural fibres.

Manufactured by Classicscan Pte Ltd Singapore
Printed in Malaysia by Times Offset (M) Sdn Bhd

Dedication

*I dedicate this book to my lovely, ever-growing
family and to the memory of my most beloved
father, whose artistic talents are already evident
in his grandchildren and great grandchildren.*

Acknowledgements

*I would like to thank Winsor & Newton for
their help in providing all the painting
materials used in this book and R K Burt &
Company for the watercolour blocks on which
all the scrapbooking backgrounds are painted.
I would also like to thank Jowett & Sowery of
Leeds for their computer ink.*

Cover
In olden days
See page 39.

Page 1
Beside the seaside
See page 30.

Opposite
A dancer's life
See page 31.

Contents

A few steps of
a dancer's life

Patricia's first trophy
Photo for White Lodge
Giselle
Nutcracker
Romeo & Juliet with
Nureyev in New York

Introduction

The idea behind this book is to introduce scrapbooking enthusiasts to the wonderful medium of watercolour. It is a new way of presenting precious photographs so that they can be enjoyed by family, friends and future generations.

Most of us have boxes full of photographs which we frequently promise to file. Scrapbooking is an excellent way of displaying them, using specially made cardstock, papers and embellishments. Some scrapbookers, though, might want to create their own paper backgrounds for their pages.

Watercolour is perfect for producing a rich variety of backgrounds; it can create moods, enhancing the themes and even the emotional content of your photographs. It can be quiet and understated or bold and exciting. The amazing thing is that the watercolour itself does this, with just a little help from you.

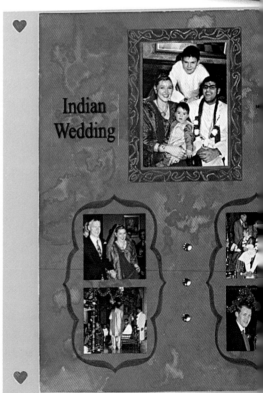

The first part of the book deals with wash effects such as blending, spattering and resist. Then you take more control of the paint and produce shapes to frame your pictures. Simple motifs such as hearts are introduced next. Then there are easy backdrops, and finally a complete picture.

Watercolour is simply coloured water, nothing more, so your brush should always be fully loaded with wash to achieve the best results. Be relaxed, play around and see what happens when you wet the paper and drop some colour on to it – magic! Have a lovely creative time producing fabulous scrapbook pages for your photographs.

Love in a hot climate

Joseph & Judith, Greece 1969

Nancy & Andy, Rome 2002

Jonathan & Ruth, Cyprus 2003

Robin & Jenny, Mexico 2002

Christopher on Brooklyn Bridge, New York

Poppa, guess where?

SCOTLAND

Julie's balcony in Vienna, Italy

Harriette and Britt Allen relaxing in Austria

People
& Places

Tiger! Tiger! Burning bright

In the forests of the night

Materials

If you are an absolute beginner, the vast array of watercolour materials can be rather confusing. For the work in this book I have used one box of paints, some tubes, four brushes and two types of watercolour paper.

Paints and brushes

Paints range from very cheap to the more expensive **Artist's watercolours**. In between these are **Student's watercolours**, which I have used throughout. They are moderately priced, have a uniform consistency and good colour range. There are fourteen pans (solid paints in little replaceable compartments) in my **compact box**, which was more than enough to achieve variety. **Tubes** of Student's watercolours are probably easier to use when mixing large washes. If you have a birthday coming up, you could drop the odd hint and get a box of tubes and a set of half pans.

I have been very specific about paint colours in my instructions, but if you do not have the ones mentioned in the text, simply use the closest colour you can find.

The best **watercolour brushes** are made from sable. I have used brushes with a blend of sable and synthetic hair, which are excellent, hardwearing and economically priced. I used the no. 10 round for washes and the no. 4 round for more detailed work; a one stroke 13mm (½in) flat and a no. 4 fan for creating different marks and textures.

You will also need some **small dishes** for mixing the washes and some **water pots**. Old plastic **film canisters** are very useful for storing leftover washes, which can be mixed later to make another colour. Washes seem to last forever when kept in an airtight container.

Student's watercolours in a box of fourteen pans, water pots, film canisters, tubes, plastic dishes and brushes.

Paper

Any **watercolour paper** must be acid free, like all scrapbooking materials, to prevent damage to your photographs.

Watercolour paper tends to cockle and distort when wet. This is a problem for scrapbooking because a buckled sheet of paper would make a useless mount for photographs. Artists stretch paper in order to prevent cockling, but this can be a lengthy process. A good alternative is to use a block of watercolour paper. This is gummed on four sides to keep the paper taut while you work. When the wash is completely dry, you slip a sharp blade between the sheets and pull it all the way round to remove the paper. These blocks are available from art shops and vary in price. I used a 23 x 30.5cm (9 x12in) 300gsm (140lb) **Not block**, excellent quality and not too expensive. 'Not' simply means that the paper was not hot pressed, so it has some surface texture.

I also used a 300gsm (140lb) **Not pad** for practising various techniques. This is essential for experimenting and testing colour. Never go straight on to the block before first trying out a colour or technique on the pad.

An ordinary **cartridge pad** will be useful for planning the design of each of your pages.

I have mounted my watercolour background sheets on to **cardstock** in toning colours. Cardstock is cut in sizes to fit scrapbooking albums, usually 30.5 x 30.5cm (12 x 12in), and comes in a huge variety of colours. It must be acid and lignin free to protect your photographs from damage.

White **mulberry tissue paper** is used for the title in one project.

Wax-coated card is ideal for creating stencils used for spattering techniques.

The Not pad used for trying out washes and techniques.

A selection of cardstock with a Not block, cartridge pad and wax-coated card.

Other materials

Art **masking fluid** is a yellow-tinted liquid rubber used to mask areas of the paper, making them resistant to water. It must be allowed to dry (usually a matter of minutes) before over-painting. Once the paint has dried, the masking fluid can be gently rubbed away using a clean finger. A firm **colour shaper** (usually used for blending and shaping in pastel and charcoal work), and a **mapping pen** are used for applying the masking fluid. The shaper is used for drawing and filling in shapes; the pen for writing. Some people use old brushes but as the fluid dries very quickly, it will almost certainly ruin the brushes unless they are dipped continually in hot soapy water.

Wax candles are used for resist techniques. An **old toothbrush** is used for spattering and natural **sea sponges** for sponging. **Polythene** and **salt** are used to create paint effects in a wet wash. A **hairdryer** can be used to speed up the paint drying process, but do not use it on masking fluid, as this can make it stick permanently to the paper.

Absorbent **kitchen paper** is useful for removing colour and for mopping up accidental spills.

A **pencil**, **sharpener**, **eraser** and **tracing paper** are used for drawing.

A **cutting mat**, **metal ruler** and quality **craft knife** are essential for cutting. I use a steel-handled knife. Straight, sharp, pointed **scissors** are also useful. Curved **cuticle scissors** are useful for cutting circles and **fancy-edged scissors** for creating decorative edges.

Various **craft punches** and **alphabet stamps** and **inkpads** are useful for decorating pages and for journaling.

A hairdryer, acetate, metal ruler, poster paint, mapping pen, colour shaper, pencil, old toothbrush, craft knife, salt, polythene, masking fluid, alphabet stamps and inkpads, printed paper and handmade paper, ordinary, cuticle and fancy-edged scissors, craft punches, a sea sponge, glue stick, photo stickers, spray adhesive, double-sided tape, bits of wax candle, an eraser, pencil sharpener and bindis.

Silver **acrylic paint** can be used for edging photograph mats.

Bindis are used for decoration. I bought them from an Indian shop, but many craft shops now supply them.

Photo stickers are used to stick down the photographs, titles and journaling. **Glue sticks** are useful for embellishments and thick cardstock labels or titles. **Photo mount** spray is used for sticking acetate. **Double-sided tape** can be used for sticking photographs or lightweight embellishments.

A **computer** is most often used for printing out titles and journaling. **Acid-free pens** are just as useful. All the photographs in this book were reproduced using a **scanner** and **printer** because many of the originals were lent by my family and I wanted to return them uncut. In this way, photographs can be enlarged or reduced to suit your page design and enhanced and retouched where necessary. Captions and borders can also be added.

I have also printed some titles on clear **acetate** so that the wash can be seen behind them.

Albums

There are three main types of scrapbooking album. **Ring-bound albums** have top-loading page protectors to put your layouts in. They cannot be extended. **Strap-bound albums** have pages connected with plastic straps. You work on the pages and then cover them with slip-over protectors. They can be extended by adding pages to the strap. **Post-bound albums** have screw posts that bind together page protectors. You put your layouts into the protectors, and you can screw in extension posts if you want to add more pages.

Most albums, cardstock and paper are 30.5 x 30.5cm (12 x 12in). All the layouts in this book were done using this size.

Techniques

All the techniques used for the scrapbook pages are shown here, and they are also described where they appear in the projects. There are two elements to the secret of success. One is planning – use your cartridge pad to jot down ideas and draw thumbnail sketches of your page designs. The second is practice – always test the colours on your watercolour pad first and always practise the technique a few times before going on to the block.

Washes

Mixing a wash

Mix a little paint with lots of water. Test the mix on your pad until you achieve the desired density of colour. Watercolour always dries lighter.

Applying a flat wash

Tilt the watercolour block by putting something level, such as a wooden prop, under the top end. Using a loaded no. 10 round brush, start at the top and work across and down, just catching the bottom of the previous line of wash each time. Reload the brush before it runs out of paint.

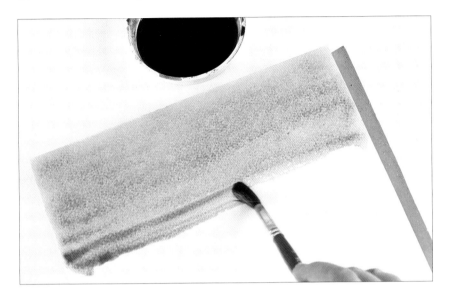

Applying a soft two-colour wash

Have two washes ready. Apply a clean water wash to the whole page, then immediately apply areas of coloured wash. You can move them around a little while they are still wet, but generally just leave them to work their own magic.

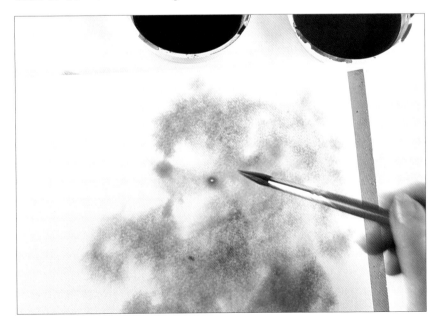

Blending

Have two washes ready. Lay the first at the top of the page, then immediately take the second wash across, allowing the two to touch and mingle. Continue down the page, alternating colours as shown.

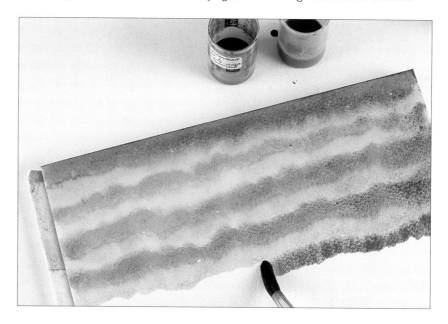

Resist

Wax resist

Use an ordinary household candle. Break or cut sections off to form sharp pieces, then write or draw as you would with a pencil. Apply a wash over the top and the image will remain white. You do not need to remove the candle wax.

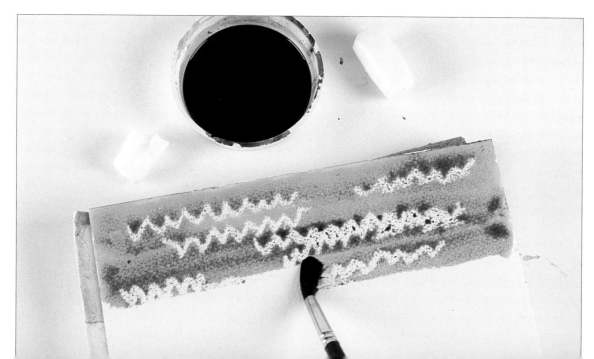

Masking fluid

1. Use the colour shaper to fill in areas. Draw a shape lightly, and use the shaper to drop some masking fluid within the image and spread it around to fill the shape.

2. Use a mapping pen to write with the masking fluid. Hold the pen diagonally and apply gentle pressure. When the nib becomes clogged with thick fluid, peel it away.

3. When the masking fluid is dry, apply a wash over the shape and the writing.

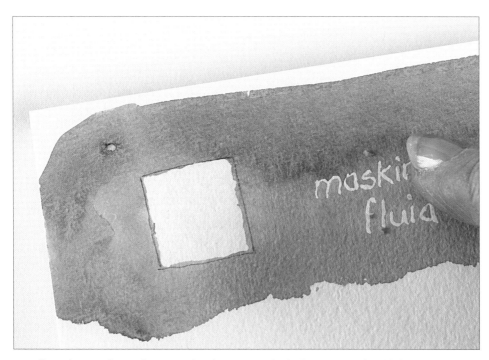

4. Allow the wash to dry completely. Use a clean finger to rub off the masking fluid.

Textures

Imprinting

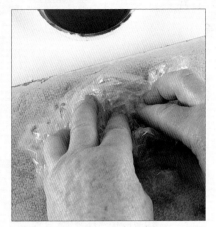

1. Press some crumpled polythene on to a wet wash.

2. Lift off the polythene to see the effect. Repeat until the desired texture is achieved.

Frosting with salt

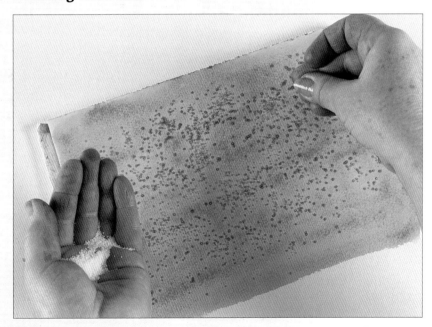

1. Sprinkle fine sea salt on to a wet wash. Each grain will absorb the colour, then release it. This makes the beautiful texture.

2. Leave the salt to dry naturally, then brush it off gently with clean fingers.

Sponging

1. Using a no. 10 brush, paint a wash on to a damp sponge. Do not dip the sponge into the wash.

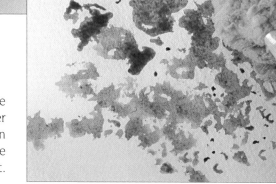

2. Press the sponge on to the watercolour block. If other colours are to be included in the same area, work from the lightest to the darkest.

'ng

1. Make a stencil from wax-coated card. Dip an old toothbrush in a wash, pull back the bristles and flick paint over the stencil.

2. Lift up the stencil to reveal the spattered design.

Leaving out colour

Speckles

Speckles are produced simply by leaving little random areas of white when applying a wash.

Highlights

Highlights are rather more contrived than speckles and are left out of the wash to give a spark of life and a three-dimensional appearance. If it helps, lightly draw the highlight before painting.

Removing colour

Using a brush

You can use a damp brush to remove paint from a dry wash. Always pat the area with kitchen paper afterwards to absorb any excess water and prevent watermarks.

Using a knife

A very sharp knife can also be used on a dry wash. The surface of the paper is lightly scuffed to give a mottled effect, which is very good for tree bark, rocks and sparkling water.

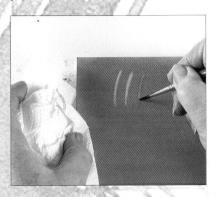 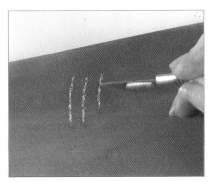

Painting

Spreading stars

Paint a wash on the paper. After a few seconds, drop some clean water into the wet wash. You can gently encourage the water to spread from the middle with the tip of your brush.

Coloured stars

Have two washes ready. Put a blob of wash on the paper. Pull the edges of the wash out using the fan brush, then immediately drop another colour into the centre.

Coloured circles

Prepare two washes. Paint a circle of clear water, then immediately touch it with alternate droplets of coloured wash. The washes will blend and eventually dry as two-colour circles.

White Winter Wonderland

This is a one-colour wash using spattered masking fluid to give the effect of snow. Practise first on your pad just to get the hang of spattering. It is only a minor catastrophe if you flick the wrong way and cover your glasses with dots, but clothes are a little more serious. Do not worry if you drop a few large blobs on the page; these can be carefully removed when the fluid has dried and then filled in with wash when the fluid has been rubbed off or, like any other little errors, covered by a photograph!

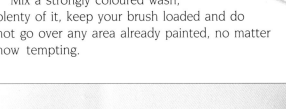

This concept is artistic licence big time because the sky would be a pale grey if it were snowing, but white against a lovely rich blue looks so much prettier. Red has been chosen as the title colour because of its prominence in the photographs.

Mix a strongly coloured wash, plenty of it, keep your brush loaded and do not go over any area already painted, no matter how tempting.

You will need

Photographs

White cardstock, 30.5 x 30.5cm (12 x 12in)

Extra white card for journaling

300gsm (140lb) Not watercolour block

300gsm (140lb) Not watercolour pad

Art (cream-coloured) masking fluid

Old toothbrush

Wooden prop to tilt block

Ultramarine watercolour

No. 10 round brush, water pots and mixing dish

Red and blue pens or computer for title and journaling

White mulberry tissue paper

Kitchen paper

Photo stickers

Glue stick

Snowflake craft punch

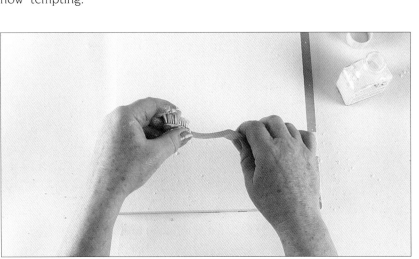

1. Dip the toothbrush into the masking fluid and proceed to thoroughly spatter the entire surface of the block, particularly round the edges. This should be dry in five minutes.

2. Mix a strongly coloured wash of ultramarine. Prop the block up a little at the top so that it is slightly tilted. Load your brush and, starting at the top, work evenly across and down, just touching the previous line of wash as you work.

3. When the wash is completely dry, use your fingers to gently rub away the spattered masking fluid.

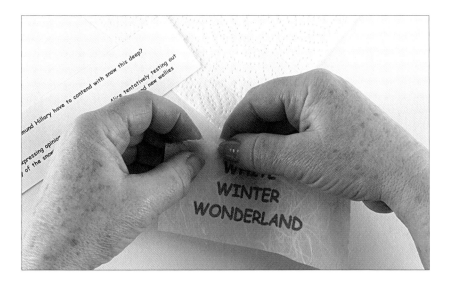

4. Print or write your journaling in blue on white card. Print or write the title in red on the mulberry tissue paper, then tear it to create soft edges. Tear a similar-sized piece of kitchen paper.

5. Position and secure the photographs using photo stickers and the journaling using glue stick. Secure the kitchen paper using a photo sticker in the centre only, then place the title on top and secure it in the same way.

Luke in Wales - did Edmund Hillary have to contend with snow this deep?

WHITE WINTER WONDERLAND

Doris (the dog) expressing opinions on the validity of the snowman

Alice tentatively testing out her brand new wellies

White Winter Wonderland

The finished page. There is something magical about looking up into a street light when the world is quiet and snow is gently falling. This simple technique of spattering with masking fluid endeavours to replicate this lovely sensation. The spattered background is mounted on snow-white cardstock and snowflake shapes punched from blue-painted card complete the picture.

The Malaysian jungle canopy

Christopher on Brooklyn Bridge, New York

Poppa, guess where?

SCOTLAND

Wonderful camel ride in fascinating Egypt

Juliet's balcony in Verona, Italy

Harriette and little Alice relaxing in Austria

People & Places

People & places

Here two colours, green representing the earth and blue the sky and sea, have been allowed to bleed into each other. A loaded brush of blue (a mixture of ultramarine and cerulean blue) is taken across the block, then immediately a loaded brush of sap green is washed underneath it, just touching. Since they are both wet, the colours mingle and sometimes tiny tree-like shapes form. Deep red cardstock brings out the brightness of the blue-green combination. The little passport embellishments were made by scanning my own passport, reducing the image and printing it on to photographic paper.

Happy school days

This layout uses the resist method. I used a wax candle to write mathematical symbols on the block, then laid a wash diagonally, allowing it to be weak or strong in areas. I chose orange, a mix of burnt sienna and cadmium red pale hue to pick up my son's hair colouring. When the wash had dried, I dropped blobs of strong colour and blew on them to give the effect of ink blots. The title was printed using a rubber alphabet and the report comments were printed on the computer.

Wonderful weddings

Family weddings are wonderful. Here I wanted a feeling of light, floating confetti. I worked down the page fairly quickly so that the colours blended. While painting the wash, I deliberately left tiny areas of white to represent the confetti. The blue, a mix of ultramarine and cerulean, and the pink, a mix of alizarin crimson and purple lake, are fairly strong. A more delicate effect could be achieved by simply adding water to reduce the intensity of the colours. Heart shapes punched from paper treated with the same washes as the background are placed on the cardstock to harmonise the design.

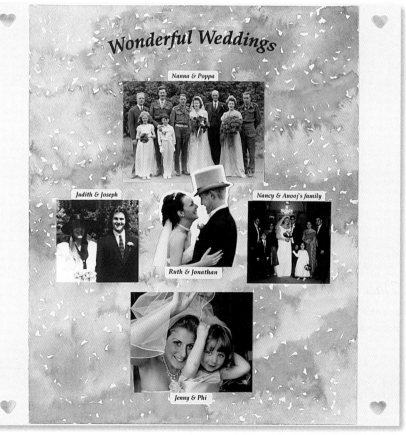

Tiger! Tiger! Burning bright

In the forests of the night

Tiger tiger

This little tiger, my youngest granddaughter, demonstrates the removal of colour. Two strengths of green were used; the dark wash was a mix of viridian and burnt umber, then for the light wash the same two colours were used with lemon yellow added. The two washes were applied so that they blended and after a few seconds a sheet of crumpled polythene was pressed on to the damp wash, then carefully removed. When the wash was perfectly dry, I drew the lines using a clean, wet brush. Kitchen paper was used immediately to pat the wet line and reduce the chance of watermarks.

23

All dressed up

A very bright page. There are three colours – alizarin crimson, cadmium red pale hue and cadmium yellow. The pale wash was laid and allowed to dry. The stars were produced by dropping generous blobs of crimson on to the block, pulling the blob out at different angles with a fan brush, then immediately dropping a blob of yellow on to the centre. The circles were made by painting circles of clean water, then dropping alternate drops of crimson and yellow into the water. I used acetate for the four captions and the title so that more of the background could be seen. Black cardstock and painted watercolour paper circles to match those on the background complete the look.

Special moments

Special moments are like little stars in our lives, and there are so many of them. The diagonal wash was worked in strips, each strip very slightly overlapping the previous dry one to give a fine definition line. Clean water was dropped on to the wet wash and, after a few seconds, the drops spread out to form star-like shapes. Some were left just as they formed, while others were pulled out using a clean, damp no. 4 brush to form star points.

Kiss Kiss

The heart motif is usually associated with Valentine's Day, engagements or weddings. But kissing at any time and any age is gorgeous. The act expresses love and affection; therefore hearts are not out of place on this page.

The size of the hearts will be determined by the size of your photographs. The heart shapes do not have to be perfectly symmetrical. Place a piece of tracing paper over the photograph and draw a heart – it really does not matter if it is misshapen – then cut out the photograph and tracing together. Practise drawing hearts on your cartridge pad if you are not confident. The little hearts are also drawn freehand (but use the template shown below if you want to), and then painted within the pencil lines, which can be erased later. The small curved highlight in each heart is made by simply leaving a gap when painting; it gives the appearance of roundness.

You will need

Photographs
Red cardstock, 30.5 x 30.5cm (12 x 12in)
300gsm (140lb) Not watercolour block
300gsm (140lb) Not watercolour pad
Wooden prop to tilt block
Alizarin crimson and purple lake watercolours
No. 10 and no. 4 round brushes, water pots and mixing dish
Pen and acetate
Tracing paper
Pencil and eraser
Straight and cuticle scissors
Photo stickers
Photo mount spray
Heart craft punch

The template for the small heart.

1. Mix a wash of alizarin crimson and purple lake. Test the colour for strength on your practice pad. Apply it to the slightly angled block using the no. 10 brush, starting at the top and working evenly down. Do not be tempted to go back over the wash – just let things happen.

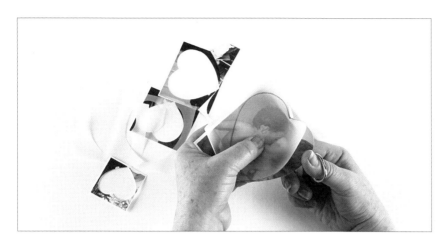

2. Having chosen your photographs, lay the tracing paper over the first and draw a heart. When you are happy with the shape, hold the two firmly together and, using the drawing as a guide, use cuticle scissors to cut them both out. Continue with the remaining pictures, making different-sized hearts.

3. Write or print the title and journaling on to acetate in curved lines. Cut them out round the curves. Arrange the photographs, title and journaling on the dried wash – do not stick them. Draw round the photographs very lightly, then lightly draw little hearts between the photographs. You can use the template to help if you want to.

4. Remove the pictures, titles and journaling from the block. Take the no. 4 brush and the same wash and paint a frame for each photograph, using the pencil lines as a guide. Fill in the little hearts, keeping within the pencil lines, which can be erased later. Leave a little curved gap in each one as a highlight.

5. When the washes are dry, rub out any pencil lines. Stick the photographs down using photo stickers, then the title and captions using photo mount spray.

Kiss kiss

Spontaneous kisses captured for ever. This is a simple flat wash with little free-drawn (or traced) motifs. The painted frames give more definition to the pictures and, because they are the same colour as the hearts, pull the design together. The background is mounted on red cardstock and the finishing touch is provided by hearts punched from watercolour paper painted with the same wash.

Beside the seaside

Two methods of resist were used for this page. I drew the motifs and traced them on to the block, then filled in the shapes with masking fluid, using a colour shaper. When the fluid had dried, I drew simple wave-like lines across the block using wax candle, then applied the blue wash. When this had dried, the fluid was rubbed off and a sand-coloured wash applied to the motifs. The minor problem with candles is that it is virtually impossible to see where you have drawn. If, when the work is dry, you discover that you have not made enough marks, scrape some of the wash away with a very sharp knife, as I did here. The templates for the motifs are shown full size below.

Oscar's first *sandy bottom experience*

Beside the Seaside

Dominic bowling for England

Poppa with the little Pinders by the chilly North Sea

A few steps of
a dancer's life

Patricia's first trophy
Photo for White Lodge
Giselle
Nutcracker
Romeo & Juliet with
Nureyev in New York

A dancer's life

This is a simple flat wash, a mix of cadmium red pale hue and alizarin crimson. The photographs were arranged so that the ballet shoe motif, with its twisting ribbon, might give a vague impression of pirouetting across the page. The shoes were painted with the same background wash but a little more paint was added to emphasise the shadows made by the twists of the ribbon and the soles of the shoes. Three of the original photographs were black and white, so I decided to remove the colour of the remaining two at the scanning stage. The template for the ballet shoe motif is shown full size here.

Muffins for a marriage

This is an example of salt frosting. A strongly coloured wash was laid on the block and immediately sprinkled with fine sea salt. The salt must be allowed to dry naturally before gently dusting it off the block with clean fingers. The muffin motifs (template shown below, full size) were drawn on to the white block and painted with the same wash. I lightly indicated the pleats in the muffin case and defined the muffin shape with a gradating wash.

Building the herb garden

On this page the photographs, journaling and motifs are positioned to give the impression of a brick structure. The blending two-coloured wash, painted on to a dry block, is pale enough not to distract from the pictures or the motifs. The motifs are very simple and stylised but I meant them to vaguely represent thyme and sage, which are now prolific in my little garden. The templates are shown above, half size. You will need to enlarge them 100% on a photocopier.

32

Little additions

This page demonstrates beautifully just how transparent watercolour paint is. The highlights also help to give authenticity to the bubbles. I used various objects to draw round and painted within the pencil line, which was erased before another bubble was painted over it (it is difficult to remove pencil once it has been painted over).

The highlights were simply omitted as each bubble was painted. On close inspection, you will see that the bubbles are paler in the centre. This is achieved by pushing the wash towards the edges as soon as it has been applied. The coloured photographs have mats cut from watercolour washes.

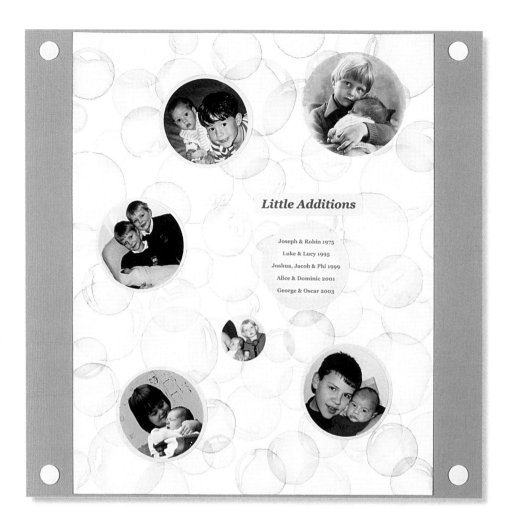

Friends

Using a simple stencil is an easy way of repeating a motif without having to re-draw it. Spattering with paint and an old toothbrush is fun because it is unpredictable, but safe, within the confines of the stencil. Here the flower stencil was cut from a specially coated wax card that prevents it from distorting when in contact with water. Cadmium yellow was used for the background wash. I first spattered with red then, when it had dried, twisted the stencil round and used a green. This was repeated with each flower head using blue with orange, then turquoise with purple. It is always best to practise this technique on your pad before going on to the block, just to see how the spatter can be affected by the pressure you put on the brush. The template for the stencil is shown here, half size. You will need to enlarge it 100% on a photocopier.

Growing Up Together

Painting little picture frames is an interesting way of presenting your photographs. I sized and cropped these photographs on the computer so that they would all fit into the same-sized frames. The secret of making the frames look three-dimensional is threefold: using two tones of the same colour; adding the little corner joints; and a slightly bevelled appearance, which is achieved by removing some of the wash with a clean, damp brush, then immediately patting the area with a piece of kitchen paper to prevent water marks.

I used a ruler and pencil to draw the frames lightly but painted them freehand. The inside of the frames will be covered by the photograph so it does not matter if the paint does not quite follow the pencil line. Do not worry if the outer line is a bit wobbly – it is the nature of watercolour. We are painting the impression of a frame and not a photographic representation.

1. Sort out and crop your chosen photographs. Measure and lightly draw the required number of frames.

2. Mix a very pale, watery wash with burnt sienna and alizarin crimson. Test the colour for strength on your practice pad. Apply it to the slightly angled block using the no. 10 brush, starting at the top and working evenly down.

3. Mix a stronger wash by adding more burnt sienna, alizarin crimson and some burnt umber to give depth. Using the no. 4 brush, paint all over the frames. When they are dry, go back and paint over two adjoining sides of each frame to achieve a deeper tone.

4. Add some more burnt umber to the wash and, starting at the top again, use the no. 4 brush to paint the corner joints.

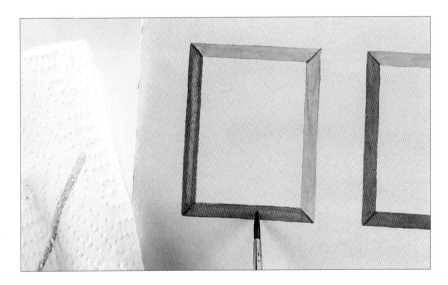

5. Run the clean, damp no. 4 brush along all four sides of the frame to remove some of the colour, avoiding the edges of the frame. Dab with kitchen paper to avoid water marks. Keep washing the brush and removing excess water on the kitchen paper. Repeat this process until a subtle highlight has formed, making the frame appear three-dimensional.

6. Position and secure the photographs and title using photo stickers.

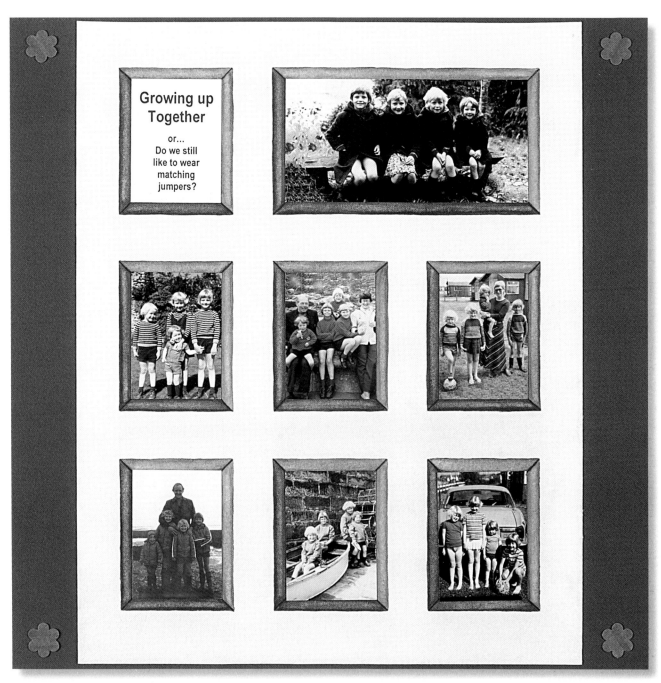

Growing Up Together

This technique is ideal for heritage layouts. These little frames are an excellent way of presenting a large number of photographs – always a nice feeling – without the result looking too cluttered. I mounted the watercolour background on warm brown cardstock and decorated the corners with flower shapes punched from paper which had been painted with the same colour as the picture frames. Glue stick was used to fix the punched flowers.

Joshua and Jacob,
first year at Prep school

...schoolboy
with his satchel
And shining
morning face...

Shakespeare

Smart schoolboys

Blue dominates this page. After sizing and cropping the photographs, the overlapping frames were lightly drawn in. The childlike writing was then written, using a mapping pen and masking fluid – one can always be selective with quotations. This one, from As You Like It, *is actually prefaced by the word* whining, *but I couldn't possibly relate that to my grandsons! When the writing had dried, a pale wash was applied to the whole page. The mottled, slightly darker wash was worked in with limited water and care was taken to keep the frame lines as straight as possible.*

In Olden Days...

A dapper Pop &
Serene Granny White
They fell in love when
She nursed him back to health
After he had been wounded
During the Great War

Lovely Nanna Pinder
Before she was married

Nanna White
As a maid of honour,
At the tender age of four
And as a gorgeous,
Confident eighteen year old
Before she joined
The Land Army

In olden days

Sepia, fawns and browns are normally used to represent the past but I thought soft pinks with a touch of silver would make a change. I first brushed clear water on to the block, then swirled brushloads of very pale (watery) alizarin crimson on to the wet paper and just let things happen. When the paper was completely dry, I removed it from the block, added water to the previous wash and produced the pale, flat pink for the mats. Fancy-edged scissors and lace punched squares suggest hints of the past. Silver acrylic paint was used for the edging and cut-outs.

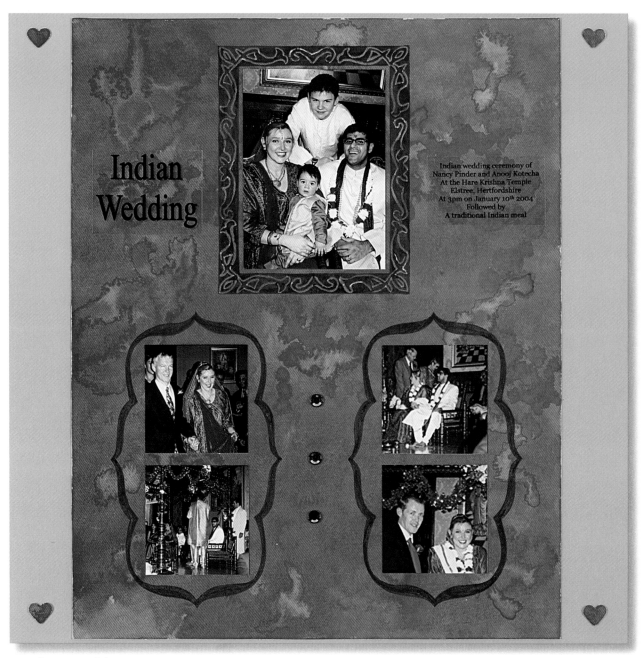

Indian Wedding

Indian wedding ceremony of
Nancy Pinder and Anooj Kotecha
At the Hare Krishna Temple
Elstree, Hertfordshire
At 3pm on January 10th 2004
Followed by
A traditional Indian meal

Indian wedding

*Red is the traditional colour for Hindu weddings, so a strong wash of alizarin crimson and
cadmium red pale hue was applied here, with water dropped on to the surface to produce lovely
random water marks. The pattern for the top frame was drawn lightly in pencil, then over-drawn
with a mapping pen and masking fluid. A strong alizarin wash was then painted over the pattern.
The masking fluid was rubbed away when it had dried. The lower frames were traced on to the
block and painted with the same strong wash. The three bindis add a touch of glamour.*

Fancy dress party

A bright cadmium yellow wash is the basis for this page. The writing and scribbled frames were produced with a colour shaper and masking fluid. Cadmium red pale hue was painted over the title and the edges blurred using a clean, wet no. 4 brush. The paint was then scribbled over the masking fluid frames and, when it had dried, the masking fluid was rubbed off. The bright lines coming away from the title were taken out of the red using a clean, damp brush, then the surface was immediately patted with kitchen paper.

Flying High

This shows another way of removing colour but here it is taken out while the wash is still wet. It is very easy and, as with most things, it will be easier still to build confidence if you have a few goes on your practice pad first. I used lightly scrunched soft kitchen paper for this technique; a damp cotton cloth can also be used.

The subject of clouds does not need to relate directly to things happening in the sky. A differently coloured, paler wash would create a lovely, light, floating impression and could be used as a backdrop for anything from babies to travelling in the spring or first communion celebrations.

The title was printed on the computer, then stuck on to the page. If you wanted to handwrite it with a yellow pen, you would have to write on a cloud because the blue sky would turn the yellow green.

You will need

Photographs

Navy blue cardstock, 30.5 x 30.5cm (12 x 12in)

300gsm (140lb) Not watercolour block

300gsm (140lb) Not watercolour pad

Ultramarine and cerulean blue watercolours

No. 10 brush, water pots and mixing dish

Kitchen paper

Metal ruler, craft knife and cutting mat

Yellow and blue pens or computer for title and captions

Photo stickers

Glue stick

Star craft punch

1. Softly crumple a few sheets of kitchen paper. Mix a strong wash with the ultramarine and cerulean blue. Test the colour for strength on your practice pad.

2. Apply the wash fairly quickly so that it does not dry before you have time to remove any colour. Start at the top and work evenly down.

3. Quickly (but as calmly as possible!) press the crumpled paper on to the wet wash to remove the colour. Dab very gently to control the shape of each cloud, being careful not to put wet wash from the paper back on to the block.

4. Leave the wash to dry. Prepare the title, then crop your chosen photographs.

5. Position and secure the title and photographs using photo stickers.

Flying High

A blue sky with a few floating cumuli just had to be the backdrop to this subject – my youngest son's surprise birthday present from his wife. The cloudy sky background was mounted on navy blue cardstock, and the star shapes were punched from a practice sheet of sky-effect watercolour paper and stuck on using glue stick.

The Pinder tree

This is an example of two-colour sponging. An artist's sponge was used to produce the foliage, but a fairly open synthetic one would make an adequate substitute. First, a watery ultramarine was applied for the sky, fading off two-thirds down the block, then a pale mix of viridian and burnt sienna were washed on to represent grass. When dry, some of the grass was taken out with clean water to accommodate the trunk. This was a mix of burnt sienna and burnt umber, one side dark blending to light on the other. To create the foliage, the sponge was dampened, brushed with the pale green, then patted on to the surface. When dry, the process was repeated with the darker green. The 13mm (½in) flat brush was used to make the branch-like lines and the pictures were taken from two wedding photographs.

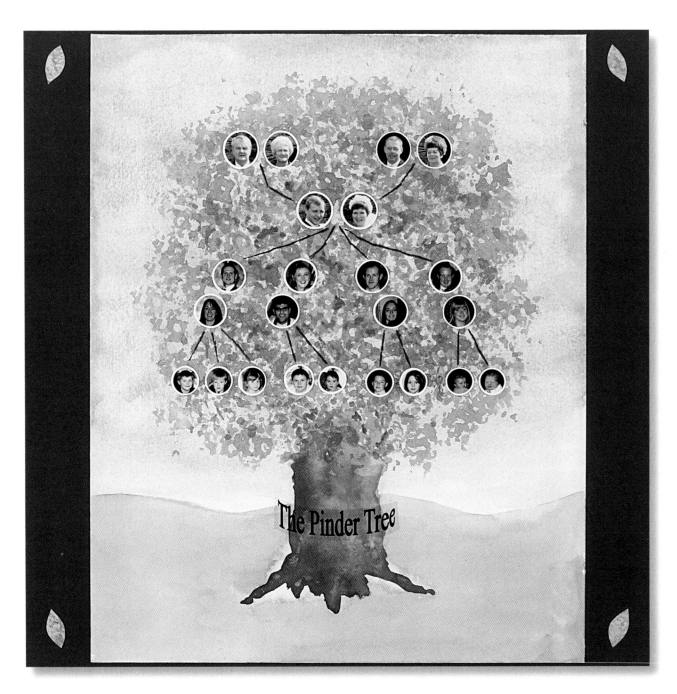

Joseph & Judith, Greece 1989
Nancy & Anooj, Rome 2002
Jonathan & Ruth, Cyprus 2003
Robin & Jenny, Mexico 2002
Love in a hot climate

Love in a hot climate

This is a basic compositional picture. First the mountain range, sea and palm trunks were very lightly drawn. Masking fluid and a colour shaper were used to block out the palm trunks. The ultramarine sky was laid, taking out a couple of wispy clouds with kitchen paper while the wash was wet. The mountains, a mix of purple lake and raw umber, were then painted. A wax candle was drawn lightly along the sea edge to give the impression of foam, then a streaky wash of cerulean blue and viridian was applied. A watery mix of cadmium yellow and yellow ochre was used for the sand. Leaving one side of the palm trunks white, burnt umber was painted down the near side. The palm fronds were painted with a 13mm (½in) flat brush and two strengths of a sap green and burnt umber mix.

Index

Beautiful bridesmaids

Beautiful bridesmaids will be in everyone's album. The soft two-coloured effect, reflecting the colours of the balloons and dresses, was made by laying a wash of clear water on the paper then adding mixtures of purple lake, ultramarine and cerulean blue at intervals and moving them round the paper with the wash brush. The daisies were punched from a sheet of watercolour paper washed with a much diluted alizarin crimson.